DATE DUE

DEMCO 38-297

Exploring Shapes

© Aladdin Books Ltd 1998
Produced by
Aladdin Books Ltd
28 Percy Street
London W1P OLD

First published
in the United States
in 1998 by
Copper Beech Books,
an imprint of
The Millbrook Press
2 Old New Milford Road
Brookfield, Connecticut 06804

Project Editor: Sally Hewitt
Editor: Liz White
Design David West Children's Book Design
Designer: Simon Morse
Photography: Roger Vlitos
Illustrator: Tony Kenyon

Library of Congress
Cataloging-in-Publication Data

King, Andrew, 1961-
Exploring shapes / by Andrew King ; illustrated by Tony Kenyon.
p. cm. — (Math for fun)
Includes index.
Summary: Games and projects introduce two-dimensional
and three-dimensional shapes, including the square, rectangle,
triangle, circle, and polygon.
ISBN 0-7613-0851-2 (lib. bdg.).
— ISBN 0-7613-0745-1 (pbk.)
1. Geometry—Juvenile literature. [1. Shape. 2. Mathematical recreations.]
I. Kenyon, Tony, ill. II. Title.
III. Series: King, Andrew, 1961-
Math for fun.
QA445.5.K53 1998   98-6805
516—dc21   CIP AC

MATH *for fun*

Exploring Shapes

Andrew King

Copper Beech Books

Brookfield, Connecticut

CONTENTS

INTRODUCTION

You can see interesting shapes everywhere. Architects use shapes to build houses, bridges, and machines. Artists make amazing patterns with shapes. You can make beautiful tessellating patterns and fascinating puzzles and games when you learn about two- and three-dimensional shapes.

Try out the amazing activities, fun games, and practical projects in this book and you can have fun learning about shapes.

● Follow the STEP-BY-STEP INSTRUCTIONS to help you with the activities.

● Use the HELPFUL HINTS for clues about the experiments and games.

● Look at MORE IDEAS for information about other projects.

1 Yellow squares mean this is an easy activity.

2 Blue squares mean this is a medium activity.

3 Pink squares mean this is a hard activity. You'll have to think extra hard!

SQUARES AND RECTANGLES

What do you know about squares? They have four corners and four sides, but do you know what is special about them? The sides are all the same length and the angles at the corners are all the same. Rectangles' corners are all the same angle and their opposite sides are the same length.

THE BLACK HOLE

1 Two players must try to cover a piece of paper with rectangles, without falling down the black hole! You need paper, colored pencils, and a ruler.

2 To make the grid for the game, fold a piece of paper in half lengthways as shown in the picture. Repeat this three more times. Unfold the paper and do the same, folding from top to bottom.

3 Unfold the paper and draw lines along the folds to make your grid. Choose any square and draw the black hole.

4 Players take turns to color a rectangle following the lines of the grid. You could draw a rectangle that takes up lots of spaces or one that takes up just one space if you like. Avoid the black hole. If you draw over the black hole you lose!

HELPFUL HINTS

● A ruler might help you to draw the sides of the rectangle straight.

● You can draw a square on the grid because a square is a rectangle, too!

MORE IDEAS

● If you are good at playing The Black Hole, try Sea Monsters!

● Make the grid again, but this time draw four sea monsters on it.

● Can you draw rectangles that avoid the hungry beasts?

TESSELLATIONS

Do you have any tiles in your house? There might be some in the kitchen or bathroom, on the walls, or on the floor. The tiles are often square shaped because they fit together easily, leaving no gaps. When a shape fits together like this we say the shape **tessellates**.

TESSELLATING TILES

You can use squares to make interesting tessellating shapes. You will need some paper, thick cardboard, a compass, tape, scissors, a pencil, and colored markers

1 Cut a square of cardboard with sides of about 2in.

2 Cut out a part of the square and move the part to the opposite side of the square like this.

3 Attach it to the other side of the square with some tape. Place your new tile in the middle of the paper and draw around it lightly with a pencil.

4 Pick up the tile and place it so it fits in with the first outline. There shouldn't be any gaps! Keep repeating this across the page until it is covered.

5 Outline the tiles with a thick marker and decorate the tiles with a bright pattern.

HELPFUL HINTS

● You can make a square with a compass. Open the arms about 2in apart. Place the point at the corner of the page (A) and make a mark with the compass along the two edges of the paper (B and C). Place the compass point on B and mark an arc, do the same on C. Where the arcs cross mark D. Use the ruler to join A, B, C, and D and cut out your square.

MORE IDEAS

● Try making more complex tile patterns by cutting out more than one part of the square.

● Make sure you move the part you have cut to line up exactly on the opposite side of the square.

THE THIRD DIMENSION

Shapes that are flat, like squares and rectangles, have two **dimensions**, length and width. Three-dimensional shapes, like cereal boxes and cans, also have height. Some boxes can be opened out and flattened. When this is done you can see the two-dimensional shapes, called faces, it is made from. The flat unfolded shape is the **net** of the box.

FISHING NETS

Find a die. How many faces does it have? What shape are they? There are six square faces. We call this shape a cube. If you could unfold the cube to make a net what would it look like?

1 Make six equal squares from cardboard — these will be the six faces of the cube. Draw a fishing net and fish on each of the faces.

2 Arrange the squares with one or more of their sides together to make a net for a cube. If your net were folded, would it make a cube?

3 Tape the squares on the plain sides and try folding the net into a cube. Does it work? If it does, unfold it again and draw a picture of the arrangement of the squares.

4 Can you find another way of arranging the squares into a net that makes a cube?

● A quick way of making a large square is to take the corner of a piece of thin cardboard and bend it over until it reaches the opposite side like this.

● Make a mark where it meets the edge then fold the small piece over so that a straight line is made across the cardboard. Cut along the line to make the square.

Same length

Cut along line

MORE IDEAS

● Draw some nets that you know can be folded to make a cube. Now draw some nets that you know will not make a cube.

● Challenge your friends to figure out just by looking at the nets whether they will make a cube.

5 There are lots of different nets that make a cube. How many can you find?

TRIANGLES

I'm sure you know what a triangle is but did you know how amazing they are? You can use them to make many shapes with any number of straight sides. Take these triangles for a "walk" and see what shapes you can make!

WALKING TRIANGLES

1 Draw a triangle with a ruler on a piece of cardboard. Cut it out carefully. Mark one of the corners with a marker on the front and back.

2 Put your triangle on a piece of paper. The marked corner stays fixed — it does not ever move from that spot. Draw around the triangle.

3 Now, flip over the triangle, keeping the marked point fixed and the edge of the outline touching the cardboard like this. Draw around the triangle again.

4 Keep repeating this until the triangles you have drawn are about to overlap. Draw around the edge of your shape with a ruler and color in the triangles carefully to make some beautiful patterns.

HELPFUL HINTS

● When you draw around your triangle, do it lightly and quickly with a pencil. If you make a mistake, it is easy to erase it later. Remember, you will be going over the lines later with markers and a ruler.

MORE IDEAS

● Don't stop drawing the triangles when they are about to overlap.

Keep walking the triangle! What happens to the shape that you make? Go on, get carried away!

MORE TRIANGLES

Did you know there are different types of triangles?

An isosceles triangle has two sides of equal length — the marks show that sides are equal.

All the sides of an equilateral triangle are the same length.

A right-angled triangle has one corner that looks like the corner of a square.

A scalene triangle has no equal sides.

TROTTO!

1 Trotto can be played by two, three, or four players. To play, make 12 cards. On each card draw a triangle, make sure you draw three of each type. Draw in the marks on the equilateral, isosceles, and right-angled triangles.

2 Find a die and cover each face with blank stickers. Write "miss turn" twice, "scalene," "isosceles," "equilateral," "right-angled" on the faces.

3 Deal out the cards. Place them on the floor face up. Take turns to throw the die. If it shows one of your triangles turn it over and pass the die to the next player.

4 The winner is the first player to turn over all their cards!

HELPFUL HINTS

● Equilateral triangle: Draw a line and open the compass to the length of the line. Put the compass point on one end of the line and draw an arc. Put the point on the other end of the line and draw another arc. Draw a line

from where the two arcs cross to each end of the line.

● Isosceles triangle: Draw a short line. Open the compass so it is longer than the line. Draw two arcs as you did above. Draw a line from where the arcs cross to each end of the line.

● Right-angled: Make a right angle measurer by folding any sized scrap of cardboard roughly in half. Fold it again so the folded edge meets itself neatly. Draw along the straight edges of your measurer then join the ends of the line with a ruler.

● Scalene: Easy! Just draw a triangle with no equal sides.

PYRAMIDS

A tetrahedron might sound like an alien from outer space, but it's not! It is a three-dimensional shape, a pyramid with four faces. What makes a tetrahedron special is that all four faces are triangles. It is also called a triangular-based pyramid. You have probably seen other pyramid shapes, like those in Egypt. Square-based pyramids have three triangular faces and one square face.

PYRAMID
SKELETONS!
Dare you attempt
the pyramid
skeleton challenge?

1 If you feel brave enough you will need some straws, scissors, and modeling clay.

2 Cut six straws to about 4in long.

3 Join three straws in a triangle with the modeling clay.

4 Now stick a straw in each of the three corners and bend them over until they meet at the top. Secure them with some more modeling clay.

- You don't need to measure each straw with a ruler to get the same length. A quick way of doing it is to cut one to the length you want, then use that straw as a measure against the other straws.

5 You have made the skeleton of a tetrahedron. Can you make the skeleton of a square-based pyramid with eight straws?

MORE IDEAS

- Try making a star skeleton. You will need 36 straws of the same length. Don't make the straws too long otherwise the skeleton might become weak. Make a cube from 12 of the straws.

- On each of the faces make a pyramid with four more straws. In no time you will have made a beautiful star!

CIRCLES

Trace around a plate on some paper and cut it out. You can find the center of the **circle** by folding it in half twice. The center is where the folds meet. Draw a line along the fold that crosses the center of a circle. This line is called the **diameter**. The length of the circle's edge is called the **circumference**.

Diameter

DRAWING DAISIES

1 You can make beautiful flower shapes by drawing circles! All you need is a compass, paper, markers, and pencils.

2 Draw a circle in the middle of a piece of paper. Pick up the compass but don't move the arms! Place the point anywhere on the circumference and draw another circle.

3 Put the point of the compass on one of the places where the two circles meet and draw the third circle.

4 Draw a fourth circle where the edge of two of the circles meet like this. Keep drawing circles until you have made a lovely pattern.

5 Now you can decorate your flower with beautiful colors and make a fabulous display!

HELPFUL HINTS

● You don't have to have a compass to make these patterns. It is easy to make your own circle drawer!

● You will need a piece of cardboard, scissors, a push pin, and a pencil. Cut out a strip of cardboard. Make a hole with the pin at each end of the cardboard. Leave the pin in the cardboard and push the pencil through the other hole. Now you can draw lots of circles!

MORE IDEAS

● Try drawing different patterns. First draw a circle then place the point of the compass on the edge and draw another circle. Draw a third circle where the two meet. Now mark all the points on the edge of the shape where two circles meet and draw three more circles. Repeat this as many times as you like. Do you notice a tessellating pattern?

STRETCHING CIRCLES

Shapes can be changed by making them bigger, smaller, and in many other ways, too. One interesting way of changing circles is to stretch them. When a circle is stretched it becomes oval or an ellipse.

MAKING FACES

1 To make faces you need more than your own face and a mirror! Find an old photograph or a picture of a face from a magazine. Make sure the face fills as much of the picture as possible.

2 Place a compass point at the center of the face and lightly draw as large a circle as possible. Cut out the circle.

3 Turn it upside down and cut lines across the circle from one side of the face to the other about six or seven times like this. You could make your cuts straight or wiggly.

4 Turn the strips face up and put them back into a circle. Now stretch them out leaving the same space between each piece and make a funny face! Stick it onto cardboard.

HELPFUL HINTS

● Pictures from magazines are often on thin paper. Make your picture stronger by sticking some cardboard to the back. Now draw the circle and cut it out.

MORE IDEAS

● Try stretching other shapes like a square or a triangle or your own made-up special shapes.

● You could try a different type of stretch like the one below.

CENTERS, SECTORS, AND CONES

Radius

When you draw a circle with a compass, the compass point is the center of the circle. The distance between the center and the edge of a circle is called the **radius**. If you draw a line from the center to the edge of the circle it will always be the same length. If two lines are drawn it looks as though a wedge of cake has been cut. This wedge is called a sector.

HATS

It is a lot of fun designing party hats! To make your hats you will need plenty of colored cardboard, markers, scissors, tape, a compass, streamers, and shapes to decorate your hats.

Sector

1 Draw a large circle on some cardboard with your compass. Now draw the radius. Draw another radius. You could make the sector either wide or narrow.

2 Cut out the circle and the sector and carefully stick the edges of the larger sector together like this. You have now made a **cone**!

HELPFUL HINTS

● To help the hats stay on your friends' heads make a small hole on the inside of the hat on each side close to the ears. Thread some elastic through the hole.

Tie a knot, to stop the elastic from slipping back through the hole, and do the same on the other side.

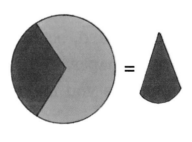

3 Last of all, decorate your hat with shapes and streamers!

MORE IDEAS

● Experiment by cutting out different sizes of sectors from the circles.

How does it change the shape of the cone?

● Cutting out a large sector will make the hat more pointed. If you cut out a small sector the hat will stay quite flat.

POLYGONS

A **polygon** is a flat two-dimensional shape with three or more straight sides. Some have special names. A pentagon has five sides. Hexagons have six sides. Heptagons have seven sides. Octagons have eight sides.

FEELY SHAPES

If you don't know the names of shapes, how well can you describe them?

1 Three or more players can play Feely Shapes. You will need some cardboard, scissors, pencils, a ruler, paper, and a bag to hide the shapes you make.

2 Draw some shapes on the cardboard. The lines must be straight but can be any length and the corners can be any angle.

Now cut them out and put them in the bag.

3 One of the players chooses a shape inside the bag. They must keep it hidden and describe it to the other players without looking at it!

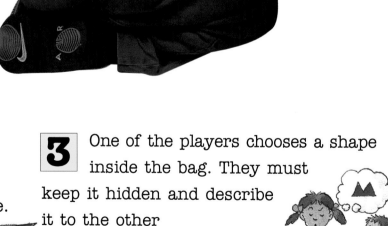

4 The other players try and draw the shape that is being described. When the other players have finished their sketches, take the shape out of the bag.

HELPFUL HINTS

● With some practice you can become very good at describing polygons.

● Try to describe the number of straight sides. Do they feel long or short?

● What do the corners of the shape feel like? Are they very pointed?

MORE IDEAS

● Try playing the same game again, but this time include shapes with curved edges, like circles and ellipses, or your own made-up shape!

5 The winner is the player that has made the best drawing of the polygon.

TANGRAMS

A tangram is an ancient Chinese shape puzzle, a little like a jigsaw. Some people think tangrams are about 2,500 years old! It is made up of five triangles, a square, and a parallelogram, which is another four-sided shape.

CATS AND DRAGONS

To make the tangram shapes you need a square of thin cardboard, markers, a ruler, and a pair of scissors.

1 Draw a grid of 16 squares on the cardboard like this. Copy the tangram shapes from below with a marker and ruler.

2 Cut out the seven shapes and mix them up. Can you put them back together to make a square? Challenge your friends and see if they can make a square!

3 Perhaps you found that easy! But can you arrange all seven shapes to make a rectangle?

4 Try making a cat shape with the tangram pieces. Remember, you must use all seven pieces.

HELPFUL HINTS

● You can make the grid for the tangram by folding the square piece of thin cardboard in half. Fold it in half again in the same direction. Unfold the square and repeat the folding from top to bottom. Your cardboard is now ready for you to copy the tangram shapes.

MORE IDEAS

● Why not make up your own tangram puzzle? Each puzzle must use all seven pieces.

● First arrange your pieces carefully on some paper. Draw around the outline lightly in pencil.

● Go over the outline again using a ruler and a marker to make it clearer. Last of all, give your puzzle a name like "the dragon" and challenge a friend to match the tangram shapes to your puzzle.

POLYHEDRA

A **polyhedron** is a three-dimensional shape. It can have any number of faces. A tetrahedron has four triangular faces and a cube has six square faces. How many faces do you think an octahedron has? That's right, eight faces!

BUILD IT!

If you look carefully around your home, you can find lots of different shapes: a box of cereal, a cylinder from the inside of a toilet paper roll, a ball, a die, or cube. Perhaps you have some wooden building blocks.

1 To play Build It! you need two of each shape. Collect about five pairs of identical shapes. If you want to, you could paint them all the same color, but check with an adult first.

2 Now sit back-to-back with a friend. Build a model with all your shapes but make sure your friend can't see!

3 Try to describe how your model is built as clearly as you can. Can your friend match your model exactly?

4 When you have both finished describing and building the model, stand up and look at how well you both did! Do the models match?

HELPFUL HINTS

● It helps to describe the position of each shape. You might say...

the cube is on top of
or
to the right of
or
underneath
or
next to
or
touching the corner of

How else can you help your partner?

MORE IDEAS
● Collect some more three-dimensional shapes and play this fun memory game. Put all the shapes on a table and let your friends have a look. Now have your friends turn away while you remove one of the shapes. Change the position of the remaining shapes then shout "ready!" Your friends now have to try and guess which shape you have taken!

COMMON SHAPES

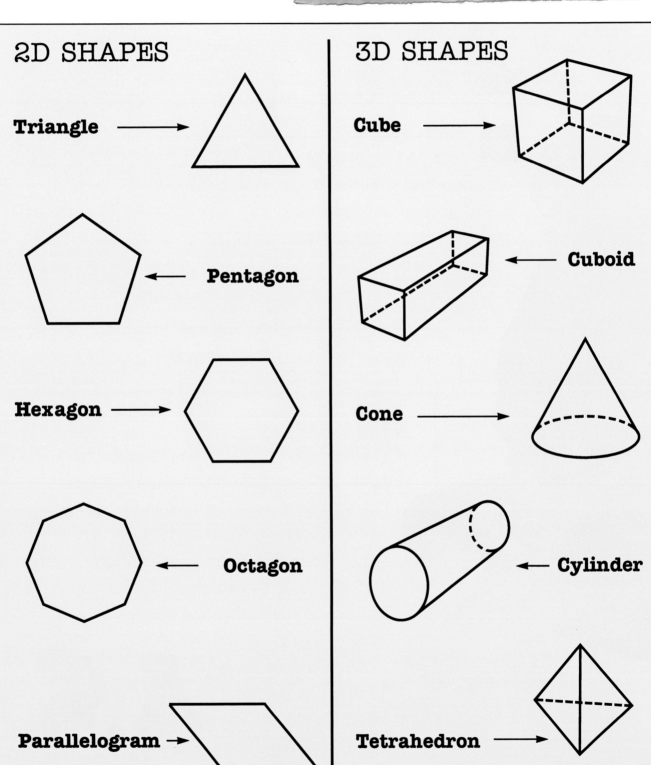

2D SHAPES

Triangle →

Pentagon ←

Hexagon →

Octagon ←

Parallelogram →

3D SHAPES

Cube →

← **Cuboid**

Cone →

← **Cylinder**

Tetrahedron →

GLOSSARY

Circle

A circle is a round shape with one curved edge. The distance from the center of the circle to any point on its edge is always exactly the same.

Circumference

The circumference is the length all the way around the edge of a circle.

Cone

A cone is a solid shape. The base it stands on is a circle. Its curved surface goes up to a point at the top.

Diameter

The diameter is a line that cuts a circle exactly in half. It goes from the edge of the circle, through the center, and to the edge on the other side.

Dimension

We use dimensions to measure shapes. Flat shapes like circles or squares are 2D because they have two dimensions. We can measure how long and how wide they are. Solid shapes like cones and cubes are 3D because they have three dimensions. We can measure how long, how wide, and how high they are.

Net

A net is a flat shape made when the sides of a solid shape, like a cube, are opened out. When the net is folded and the sides are joined together it makes a solid shape again.

Polygon

A polygon is any flat shape that has three or more straight sides. A square, a triangle, and a rectangle are all polygons.

Polyhedron

A polyhedron is any solid shape that has four or more flat sides called faces. A cube is a polyhedron with six faces. An octahedron is a polyhedron with eight faces.

Radius

The radius is the distance from the center to the edge of a circle. Any straight line drawn from the center to the edge of a circle is called a radial line.

Tessellation

A tessellation is made when lots of flat shapes are fitted together in a repeating pattern with no gaps between them.

INDEX